Heinemann First
ENCYCLOPEDIA

Volume 7

Lif-Mot

Heinemann Library
Chicago, Illinois

© 1999, 2006 Heinemann Library
a division of Reed Elsevier Inc.
Chicago, Illinois

Customer Service   888–454–2279

Visit our website at www.heinemannlibrary.com

Series Editors: Rebecca and Stephen Vickers, Gianna Williams
Author Team: Rob Alcraft, Catherine Chambers, Sabrina Crewe, Jim Drake, Fred Martin, Angela Royston, Jane Shuter, Roger Thomas, Rebecca Vickers, Stephen Vickers

This revised and expanded edition produced for Heinemann Library by Discovery Books.
Photo research by Katherine Smith and Rachel Tisdale
Designed by Keith Williams, Michelle Lisseter, and Gecko
Illustrations by Stefan Chabluk and Mark Bergin

Originated by Ambassador Litho Limited
Printed in China by WKT Company Limited

10 09 08 07 06
10 9 8 7 6 5 4 3 2 1

Library of Congress Cataloging-in-Publication Data

Heinemann first encyclopedia.
     p.   cm.
     Summary: A fourteen-volume encyclopedia covering animals, plants, countries, transportation, science, ancient civilizations, US states, US presidents, and world history
     ISBN 1-4034-7114-2 (v. 7 : lib. bdg.)
     1. Children's encyclopedias and dictionaries.
   I. Heinemann Library (Firm)
   AG5.H45 2005
   031—dc22   2005006176

Acknowledgments
Cover: Cover photographs of a desert, an electric guitar, a speedboat, an iceberg, a man on a camel, cactus flowers, and the Colosseum at night reproduced with permission of Corbis. Cover photograph of the Taj Mahal reproduced with permission of Digital Stock. Cover photograph of an x-ray of a man reproduced with permission of Digital Vision. Cover photographs of a giraffe, the Leaning Tower of Pisa, the Statue of Liberty, a white owl, a cactus, a butterfly, a saxophone, an astronaut, cars at night, and a circuit board reproduced with permission of Getty Images/Photodisc. Cover photograph of Raglan Castle reproduced with permission of Peter Evans; J. Allan Cash Ltd., pp. 13, 18, 30; C. Borland/PhotoLink, p. 41; Bridgeman Art Library, pp. 6 top, 32; Flip Chalfant/The Image Bank, p. 31; John Cleare Mountain Camera, p. 20; Trevor Clifford Photography, p. 24 bottom; Chris Honeywell, p. 27 top; Bruce Coleman/Alain Compost, p. 19 bottom; Corbis, p. 7; Jeff Foot, p. 38 bottom; Michael Holford/British Museum, p. 9 bottom; Hulton Getty, p. 48 bottom; The Hutchison Library/Bernard Regent, p. 44; Waina Cheng, p. 10 top; J.A.L. Cooke, p. 45 bottom; Kenneth Day, p. 21 bottom; Michael Fogden, p. 25; David C. Fritts, p. 40 bottom; Mike Hill, p. 40 top; Kent Knudson/PhotoLink, p. 37; Zig Leszczynski, p. 34 bottom; Renee Lynn, p. 8 top; Fred McConnaughey, p. 38 top; C. McIntyre/PhotoLink, p. 17; John Mitchell, p. 47 top; Lloyd Nielsen, p. 21 top; Stan Osolinski, p. 43; Keith Ringland, p. 33; Norbert Rosing, p. 8 bottom; Frithjof Skibbe, p. 46; Michael R. Stoklos, p. 6 bottom; Survival Anglia/Doug Allan, p. 15; K.G.Vock, p. 47 bottom; Barrie E. Watts, p. 19 top; W. Wisniewski, p. 10 bottom; Science Photo Library/David Guyon, p. 27 bottom; Pekka Parvianen, p. 29 bottom; John Sandford, p. 29 top; Scenics of America/PhotoLink, pp. 23, 35; S.Solum/PhotoLink, p. 22; Stock Market, p. 5 bottom; Tony Stone Worldwide/Byron Jorjorian, p. 5 top; Reg Watson, p. 26; Randy Wells/Stone, p. 11; Ted Wood/The Image Bank, p. 36; Zefa, p. 48 top.

Welcome to
Heinemann First Encyclopedia

What is an encyclopedia?

An encyclopedia is an information book. It gives the most important facts about many different subjects. This encyclopedia has been written for children who are using an encyclopedia for the first time. It covers many of the subjects from school and others you may find interesting.

What is in this encyclopedia?

In this encyclopedia, each topic is called an *entry*. There is one page of information for every entry. The entries in this encyclopedia explain

- animals
- plants
- dinosaurs
- countries
- geography
- history
- world religions
- music
- art
- transportation
- science
- technology
- states
- famous Americans

How to use this encyclopedia

This encyclopedia has thirteen books called *volumes*. The first twelve volumes contain entries. The entries are all in alphabetical order. This means that Volume 1 starts with entries that begin with the letter A and Volume 12 ends with entries that begin with the letter Z. Volume 13 is the index volume. It also has other interesting information.

Here are two entries that show you what you can find on a page:

The "see also" line tells you where to find other related information.

This is the letter that the entry starts with.

Fact boxes give you details about the topic.

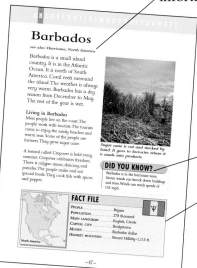

Did You Know? boxes have fun or interesting bits of information.

The Fact File tells you important facts and figures.

Life Cycle

see also: Flower, Metamorphosis

A life cycle is all the stages in the life of an animal or plant. A life cycle includes the start of life, the process of growing, having young, and then dying. Different living things have different stages in their life cycles.

Plant life cycle

A flowering plant starts its life cycle as a seed. The baby plant grows in the seed. The baby plant grows leaves and roots. It gets bigger. The new plant flowers. Its male pollen transfers to the female part of the flower. Then a new fruit with a seed grows.

DID YOU KNOW?

- Most insects have four stages to their life cycle: egg, larva, pupa, adult.
- Some insects, like grasshoppers, have only three stages: egg, nymph, adult.
- Amphibians have three stages: egg, tadpole, adult.
- Reptiles and birds lay eggs that hatch. The young grow into adults.

Human life cycle

Humans have a life cycle. It is like the life cycle of most other mammals. A human starts as an egg in a female's body. The fertilized egg grows into a baby inside the mother. This takes about 40 weeks. The parents care for the baby after he or she is born. The newborn baby is fed on milk. The baby grows. It begins to eat regular food.

the human life cycle

Light

see also: Color, Energy, Sun

Light is a form of energy. Light helps us to see. We can only see things when light bounces off them and into our eyes.

The sun and light

Light on Earth comes from the sun. All food eaten on Earth needed light from the sun at some point. Other kinds of fuel also needed sunlight at some time. Wood and gas formed from plants that grew in sunlight. Electricity is made using fuel that comes from plants that grew in sunlight.

Big cities are lit up with bright lights at night.

The sun is the source of all Earth's light energy.

How light works

Light always travels in straight lines. Nothing travels faster than light. The sun is 93 million miles from Earth. It only takes eight minutes for the light from the sun to travel to Earth. Light bounces off shiny surfaces. It bounces off mirrors and polished metal. This is called reflection. Rays of light bend when they pass through water or clear glass. This is called refraction.

Lightning

see also: Electricity, Weather

Lightning is a giant electric spark. It makes a bright flash of light in the sky. Thunder is the noise that follows the lightning. Thunder is heard because lightning heats the air as it moves through it. Light moves faster than sound. That is why we see the lightning flash and then we hear the thunder.

What causes lightning?

Lightning happens when energy in clouds turns into electrical energy. Lightning strikes when the electrical energy jumps to the ground or to another cloud. Lightning sometimes strikes buildings and tall trees. Tall buildings are usually safe from lightning. The tops of tall buildings have lightning conductors. This sends the electric energy down a thick wire into the ground.

BENJAMIN FRANKLIN (1706–1790)

Benjamin Franklin was an American scientist and politician. He flew a kite in a thunderstorm to show that lightning was electricity. The lightning struck the kite. It came down the wet string. This was very dangerous. He was lucky not to have been killed.

STAY SAFE!

If you are caught in a thunderstorm:
- Don't stay in the open or on hills.
- Find shelter inside a building or a car, *not* under trees.
- If you are swimming or boating, get out of the water and find shelter.
- Don't talk on the telephone unless it is a cellular phone with no wires.

Cloud-to-ground lightning is the most familiar.

Lincoln, Abraham

see also: Civil War

Abraham Lincoln was the 16th president of the United States of America. He kept the United States united by winning the Civil War. He freed African American slaves in the South.

Abraham Lincoln

Young Lincoln

Lincoln grew up in Kentucky and Indiana. Lincoln helped his father chop trees and farm. When there was time, he read books and went to school.

When he was older, Lincoln moved to Illinois. He learned to be a lawyer. He worked in government, too. He became famous for arguing against slavery. Southern states still used slaves to farm the land.

Lincoln becomes president

Lincoln was elected president in 1860, just before the Civil War started. In 1863, Lincoln issued the Emancipation Proclamation. The proclamation said slaves in the South should be freed. The Union defeated the South in 1865. A few days later, Lincoln was shot and killed while watching a play.

President Lincoln is pictured here on the battlefield with his generals.

FACT FILE

DATE OF BIRTH	February 12, 1809
BIRTHPLACE	Hardin County, Kentucky
DATE OF DEATH	April 15, 1865
PLACE DIED	Washington, D.C.
PRESIDENTIAL NUMBER	16
DATES IN OFFICE	1861–1865
POLITICAL PARTY	Republican
VICE PRESIDENTS	Hannibal Hamlin, Andrew Johnson
FIRST LADY	Mary Lincoln

Lion

see also: Africa, Cat, Mammal

A lion is a mammal. It is a large member of the cat family. Most lions live on the hot, grassy plains of Africa. A few lions live in India. Lions are strong, fast hunters. They sleep or rest about 20 hours a day.

LION FACTS

COLOR	light brown
LENGTH	up to 9 feet
WEIGHT	up to 400 lbs.
STATUS	common
LIFE SPAN	about 20 years
ENEMIES	cheetahs, hyenas, people

Lion families

A male is called a lion. A female is called a lioness. Baby lions are called cubs. A lioness will have two or three cubs at a time. Lion families live together in a group called a pride. The pride lives and hunts in one place. This place is called their territory.

a lion

sharp teeth for eating meat

hairy mane on male lions to look fierce and to protect them when fighting

sharp claws for hunting

strong legs for running in short, fast bursts

A lioness always watches for enemies that might attack her cubs.

MEAT EATER

A lion can eat 88 pounds of meat at one meal. The lion then spends several days sleeping off the meal. Lions usually hunt for animals such as zebra, wildebeest, and antelope.

Literature

see also: Drama, Poetry, Story

Literature is writing that is meant for other people to read. Literature may be stories, plays, poetry, or information. Some languages have no written form. They have no literature.

Literature is recorded in books, tapes, videos, and CDs.

The first literature

People have always used literature for two main reasons. First, they wrote down what had happened. They recorded their history. Second, people used writing to record stories, poems, and messages for entertainment.

Literature today

Literature grew into many forms as more people learned to read and write. Many writers wrote books. The books are filled with stories, drama, and poetry. People also watch plays in theaters. They listen to cassette tapes of stories and plays. Many TV programs and videos are works of literature. Today new literature can also be found on the Internet.

DID YOU KNOW?

The earliest form of writing that did not use pictures was called cuneiform. It was invented in Sumer in the Middle East about 4,000 years ago.

Cuneiform writing was made on clay tablets. This was the first literature.

Lizard

see also: Reptile

The lizard is a reptile. There are many kinds of lizards all over the world. Most lizards are small. A few, like monitor lizards, are large. The Komodo dragon is ten feet long. Some lizards climb trees. Other lizards live on the ground.

LIZARD FACTS

NUMBER OF KINDS	3,700
COLOR	usually greenish-brown
LENGTH	5 inches to 10 feet
WEIGHT	2 oz. to 132 lbs.
STATUS	some are rare or threatened
LIFE SPAN	6 to 50 years
ENEMIES	snakes, birds, larger lizards

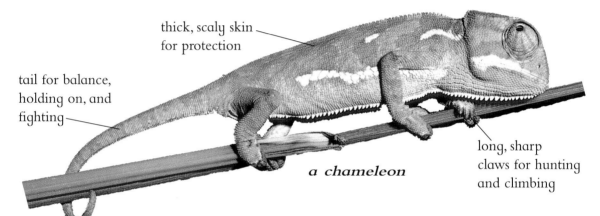

thick, scaly skin for protection

tail for balance, holding on, and fighting

a chameleon

long, sharp claws for hunting and climbing

This marine iguana baby rides on its mother's back when she climbs.

Lizard families

Some female lizards lay their eggs in soil. The soil needs to be warm to keep the eggs at the right temperature. The babies hatch after a few weeks. Other lizards keep the eggs inside them until the eggs are ready to hatch.

PLANT, INSECT, AND MEAT EATER

Lizards use their tongues to taste the air as they look for food. Most lizards eat insects and plants. Large lizards eat mammals.

Louisiana

see also: United States of America

Louisiana is a state in the southern United States of America. The state's southern border is on the Gulf of Mexico. The land is low in most of the state. The weather in Louisiana is hot and wet. Sometimes there are hurricanes.

Life in Louisiana

Most people in Louisiana live and work in cities. Many people work in shipping. Others buy and sell the goods that are shipped. Outside of the cities, farmers grow rice, sweet potatoes, and sugar cane. Fish farmers raise catfish and crayfish in ponds. People work off the shore of Louisiana, too. They catch fish and pump oil and gas out of the Gulf of Mexico.

The largest city in Louisiana is New Orleans. It is a busy port on the Mississippi River. The first people that

DID YOU KNOW?

Thousands of alligators live in Louisiana's southern swamps. In 1987, eighteen white baby alligators were found. There are no other known white alligators in the world.

A crowd celebrates Mardi Gras on Royal Street, in New Orleans.

lived in the city were settlers from France and slaves from Africa. The city still has strong French and African traditions. The New Orleans Mardi Gras festival is famous all over the world.

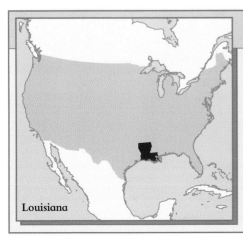

Louisiana

FACT FILE

BECAME A STATE	1812 (18th state)
LAND AREA	43,562 square miles (33rd largest land area)
POPULATION	4,496,334 (24th most populated state)
OTHER NAME	Pelican State
CAPITAL CITY	Baton Rouge

Lung

see also: Air, Human Body, Oxygen

Lungs are organs. People and animals use lungs for breathing. Lungs breathe in oxygen from the air. Lungs breathe out carbon dioxide.

Breathing

Breathing in air is called inhaling. Breathing out is called exhaling. Air is inhaled through the nose and mouth. The muscles in the chest push the air in and out of the lungs. Special hairs in the nose catch dust so it doesn't get to the lungs. The air goes down the windpipe into the lungs. The air goes through smaller and smaller tubes in the lungs.

At the end of the small tubes are many tiny air sacs called alveoli. Blood goes to the alveoli. Blood collects oxygen from the lungs. Blood gets rid of carbon dioxide.

Lung problems

Dirt and pollution can harm the lungs. Coughing is caused by the lungs squeezing together to get rid of the dirt inside.

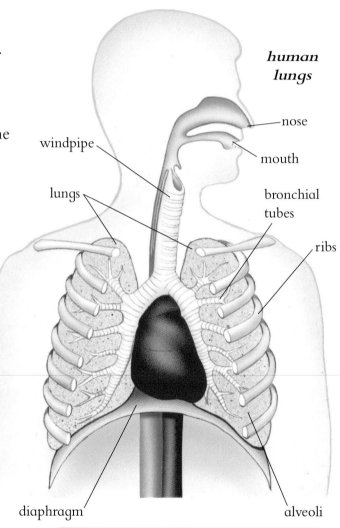

human lungs

nose

windpipe

mouth

lungs

bronchial tubes

ribs

diaphragm

alveoli

DID YOU KNOW?

If the alveoli from both lungs of an adult were flattened out, they would cover a tennis court.

STAY HEALTHY!

Keep your lungs healthy by never smoking cigarettes. Wear a mask when you do a dusty job. Try not to walk along main roads where you will breathe in exhaust fumes from cars, buses, and trucks.

Luxembourg

see also: Europe

Luxembourg is one of the smallest countries in Europe. It is mostly hills and high, flat land. One-third of the country has forests. The rest of the land is used for growing grass or crops. The summer is warm. The winter can be cold and snowy.

Living in Luxembourg

Almost all of the people work in the towns and cities. Factories make steel, glass, car tires, and chemicals. Most people work in banks and other office jobs.

Luxembourg has a royal family. It is headed by the Grand Duke. Tourists come to Luxembourg to visit old castles and to see the landscape.

This is the flower market in Luxembourg.

DID YOU KNOW?

Luxembourg has 100 percent literacy. That means everyone can read and write.

Europe

FACT FILE

PEOPLE	Luxembourgers
POPULATION	462 thousand
MAIN LANGUAGES	Letzeburgesch, French, German
CAPITAL CITY	Luxembourg
MONEY	Euro
HIGHEST MOUNTAIN	Buurgplaatz—1,835 feet
LONGEST RIVER	River Moselle—320 miles

Machine, Simple

see also: Energy

A machine helps people to do work quickly or easily. A machine can push or pull. A machine can turn a small movement into a big movement, or turn a big movement into a small movement. Six simple machines are what make all big machines work.

lever

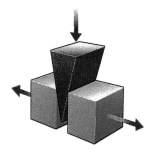

wedge

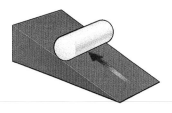

ramp

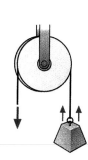

pulley

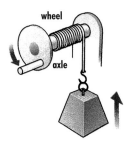

wheel

screw

These are six different types of simple machines.

DID YOU KNOW?

Playground equipment such as slides, swings, and see-saws are simple machines.

Madagascar

see also: Africa, Island

Madagascar is an island country. It is off the east coast of Africa. It is the world's fourth biggest island. There are mountains in the middle of Madagascar. Most of the low land and rivers are in the west. There are some rain forests. There are coral reefs along the east coast. The weather is mostly hot and wet.

This is the fruit and vegetable market in the city of Mahajanga.

Living in Madagascar

About three-fourths of the people live in the rural areas. They work on farms. Farmers grow rice, vegetables, and fruit. People who live on the coast go fishing. People grow or catch the food they eat. Rice and vegetables are their main foods. Most food is cooked with hot spices, peppers, and strong sauces. Coffee, cloves, and vanilla are also grown. They are sold to other countries.

DID YOU KNOW?

Madagascar is important as a home for wildlife. There are 150 thousand animals on the island that are not found anywhere else in the world. One of these animals is the lemur. It is related to the monkey.

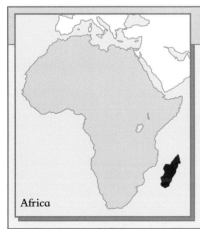

Africa

FACT FILE

PEOPLE	Malagasy
POPULATION	about 17 million
MAIN LANGUAGES	Malagasy, French
CAPITAL CITY	Antananarivo
MONEY	Malagasy franc
HIGHEST MOUNTAIN	Mount Maromokotro—9,439 feet
LONGEST RIVER	River Mangoky—348 miles

Magnet

see also: Metal

A magnet is a piece of metal. It is usually made of iron or steel. A magnet pulls another metal towards it. Every magnet has two ends. They are called poles. One pole of a magnet is pulled towards Earth's North Pole. This is called the magnet's north pole. The other end of the magnet is called the magnet's south pole.

How magnets work

If the ends or poles of two magnets are brought close to each other and they are the same poles, the magnets will push each other away. This is called repulsion. If the two poles are different, then the magnets will pull toward each other. This is called attraction.

DID YOU KNOW?

A magnet can be used to tell if a can is made from steel or aluminum. Steel cans will stick to a magnet. Aluminum cans will not stick.

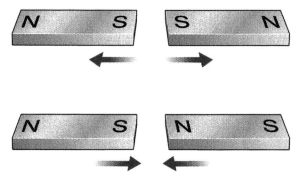

The arrows show that like poles repel and opposite poles attract.

How magnets are used

- A compass has a magnetic needle. It spins to point to Earth's North Pole.
- Magnets can be used as door catches.
- Recording tapes and computer disks are magnetic. There are millions of tiny magnets mixed into the plastic.
- Radios, televisions, and stereo systems have magnets in the speakers where the sound comes out.
- Hospitals use magnets in a machine that takes pictures of the inside of human bodies. This is called MRI.

One end of a horseshoe-shaped magnet is the south pole. The other end is the north pole.

Maine

see also: United States of America

Maine is a state in the northeastern United States of America. It is farthest east of all the states. In Maine, there are mountains, lakes, and beaches. Nearly all of the state is forested. There are many deep harbors along Maine's coast. Winters are very cold with lots of snow. Maine has over 2,000 islands along its shore and on its lakes.

Life in Maine

Lots of trees in Maine are cut for lumber. The trees are pine, spruce, and fir. Maine is one of the world's largest producers of wood pulp. The pulp is made from the trees grown in the state. The pulp is turned into paper products.

Farming and fishing are also important industries. Farmers grow apples and

Camden, Maine is set alight by the colors of the autumn.

DID YOU KNOW?

Maine was part of Massachusetts from 1691 until 1820. In that year, it separated from Massachusetts to become a state in its own right.

potatoes. They produce chickens, eggs, and milk. Nearly all the nation's blueberries come from Maine. Maine's fishing boats catch 90 percent of the lobsters in the United States.

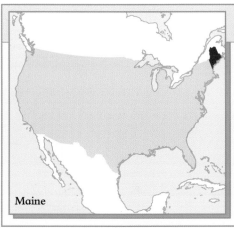

Maine

FACT FILE

BECAME A STATE... 1820 (23rd state)

LAND AREA......... 30,862 square miles
(39th largest land area)

POPULATION 1,305,728
(40th most populated state)

OTHER NAME ...... Pine Tree State

CAPITAL CITY ...... Augusta

Malaysia

see also: Asia, Rain Forest

Malaysia is a country with two parts. One part of the country is on the southeast tip of Asia. The other part is on the northern part of the island of Borneo. Both parts of Malaysia are mostly mountains and forests. The climate is hot and wet.

DID YOU KNOW?

Malaysian villages are called *kampungs*. The houses in them are made of wood. The roofs are made from palm leaves.

These women are drying cuttlefish to sell as food.

Living in Malaysia

Half of the people live in the rural areas. The farms grow rice, cocoa, and oil palms. People living by the coasts catch fish. There are many trees in the Malaysian rain forest. Some are cut down for wood. Other trees are tapped for their rubber sap. Malaysia also has factories which make cars, electronic products, and other things.

The people of Malaysia are Malays, Chinese, and people from India. Malaysia's food, houses, and clothing come from these three cultures. The most well-known Malay food is *satay*. This is grilled meat on a stick. It is usually served with spicy peanut sauce.

Asia

FACT FILE

PEOPLE	Malays or Malaysians
POPULATION	about 23 million
MAIN LANGUAGES	Bahasa Malaysia, English, Chinese
CAPITAL CITY	Kuala Lumpur
MONEY	Ringgit
HIGHEST MOUNTAIN	Kinabalu—13,459 feet
LONGEST RIVER	River Rajang—350 miles

Mammal

see also: Animal, Vertebrate

Mammal is the name given to a group of animals. There are more than 4,000 different kinds of mammals.

What makes a mammal?
All mammals have hair or fur. Most mammal babies are born alive out of the mother. Mammals feed on their mother's milk when they are born. Mammals make heat using energy from the food they eat. They are warm-blooded animals.

The smallest mammal is the shrew. It weighs less than one tenth of an ounce.

Where do mammals live?
Mammals have lived on Earth since the time of the dinosaurs. Mammals live everywhere. They live on the ground, in the trees, and in the water. Some mammals, called bats, can even fly. Each mammal's body is different. Its body fits its way of life. For example, polar bears have thick, warm coats of white fur. They live in the freezing, snowy Arctic.

DID YOU KNOW?
The largest living mammal is the blue whale. It weighs more than 110 tons and is 102 feet long.

Only two mammals lay eggs. They are the spiny anteaters, like the one shown here, and the platypus.

SKYVIEW ELEMENTARY SCHOOL
5021 E. 123rd Avenue
Thornton, CO 80241

Map

A map is a drawing of land as it would look from above. A map that shows the details of a very small area is called a plan. Maps of the seas and oceans are called charts.

Using maps

Some maps only show roads. They help people travel from one place to another. Some maps are weather maps or maps of the stars in the sky. Maps can be bound in a book called an atlas. Maps can also be put on large sheets of paper. The paper can be folded and carried around. A globe is a round map of the earth.

People use maps to find their way around unfamiliar places.

What is on a map?

All maps have three special things. They have a compass point. The compass point shows the north, south, east, and west directions on the map. They have a distance scale. The scale shows how far it is from one place to another on the map. They have a key or legend. The key or legend gives the meanings of all the symbols on the map.

N
W · E
S

0   .1
(miles)

fields
woods
river
roads
buildings
bridge

This simple map shows a river, roads, and some buildings.

Marsupial

see also: Australia, Kangaroo, Koala, Mammal, Opossum

Marsupials are mammals. A female marsupial has a pocket called a pouch. The babies live in the pouch. Kangaroos and koalas are marsupials. Marsupials are found in Australia, Papua New Guinea, North America, and South America.

MARSUPIAL FACTS

NUMBER OF KINDS	250
LARGEST	red kangaroo can weigh up to 198 lbs.
SMALLEST	pilbra ningaui—much less than one ounce
FASTEST	kangaroos can bound along at 37 mph

Marsupial babies

All marsupial babies are born very small, hairless, and blind. A newborn marsupial baby crawls through the mother's fur. It crawls into her pouch. The baby stays in the pouch. It drinks milk. It grows until it is big enough to live outside of the pouch.

Baby kangaroos are called joeys. They are less than one inch long when they are born. When the joey gets bigger, it hops in and out of its mother's pouch. Opossum babies ride on their mother's back when they get too big to be in the pouch.

The brush-tailed possum is a marsupial from Australia. It is related to the American opossum.

The kangaroo joey lives in its mother's pouch. This joey will soon be too big to get in and out of the pouch.

Maryland

see also: United States of America, Washington, D.C.

Maryland is a state in the eastern United States of America. In the east, the state is divided by the large Chesapeake Bay. The western part of the state is in the Appalachian Mountain chain. Around the bay, the weather is mild. The winters are cooler in the west.

Many tourists visit Baltimore's waterfront.

Life in Maryland

Most people in Maryland live in towns and cities in the central part of the state between Baltimore and Washington, D.C. Baltimore is the largest city in Maryland. It is a busy port. It has one of the world's largest natural harbors in Chesapeake Bay.

People in Baltimore and other Maryland towns work in stores and other businesses. Many people

DID YOU KNOW?

Chesapeake Bay produces lots of seafood. Maryland's fishermen and women harvest crab, clams, oysters, and several kinds of fish.

commute out of the state to work in government offices in Washington, D.C. Other people work in factories. The state's factories produce steel, metal products, and electronic equipment. Some factories process and pack seafood.

Maryland

FACT FILE

BECAME A STATE	1788 (7th state)
LAND AREA	9,774 square miles (42nd largest land area)
POPULATION	5,508,909 (19th most populated state)
OTHER NAMES	Free State, Old Line State
CAPITAL CITY	Annapolis

Massachusetts

see also: American Revolution,
Colonial America

Massachusetts is a state in the northeastern United States of America. The state has a rocky coastline in the east. To the west, there are hills, mountains, and farmland. Summers in Massachusetts are warm. The winters are cold and snowy, especially in the mountains.

Cape Cod is a popular vacation spot in Massachusetts.

DID YOU KNOW?

New England is made up of Connecticut, Maine, Massachusetts, New Hampshire, Rhode Island, and Vermont.

In the past

Many important things happened in Massachusetts. The first college in North America, Harvard University, was founded in 1636. The American Revolution started in Massachusetts in 1775. In the early 1800s, another revolution began in Massachusetts. Textile mills at Lowell brought the Industrial Revolution to the United States.

Life in Massachusetts

Today, factories in Massachusetts produce industrial and electronic equipment. Farmers grow fruit, flowers, and vegetables. Tourists come to visit historic sites. They also visit beaches, theaters, and art galleries on Cape Cod.

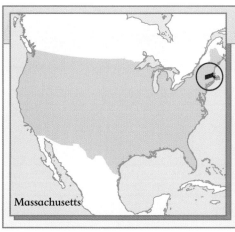
Massachusetts

FACT FILE

BECAME A STATE...	1788 (6th state)
LAND AREA.........	7,840 square miles (45th largest land area)
POPULATION	6,433,422 (13th most populated state)
OTHER NAMES	Bay State, Old Colony State
CAPITAL CITY	Boston

Matter

see also: Temperature

Matter makes up everything around us. All matter on Earth is in one of three forms. These forms are solid, liquid, and gas.

Solids, liquids, and gases

- Solids keep their shape and size. Solids cannot be squashed into a smaller space or stretched into a bigger space.
- All liquids can be poured. Liquids change their shape to fit the container into which they are poured.
- Gases can change their shape. They spread out to fill the space they are in.

Most matter can be in any of the three forms at different times. For example, frozen water is ice. That is a solid. Water at temperatures between 32°F and 212°F is a liquid. Water that is heated to more than 212°F turns into steam. Steam is a gas.

DID YOU KNOW?

All matter is made of very small particles. The particles are too small to see. These particles are called atoms. Most matter is made up of different atoms.

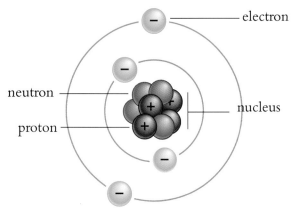

electron

neutron

nucleus

proton

the parts of an atom

Here is water in its three forms—steamy gas, liquid water, and solid ice.

Maya

see also: Aztecs, Hieroglyphics, Incas, Pyramid

The Maya were a Native American people. They lived about 1,500 years ago. The Maya ruled parts of what is now Central America. The Maya took over many small groups of people. They formed one big country. This was called the Mayan Empire. The Maya were powerful between A.D. 300 and A.D. 900.

What were the Maya like?

The Maya were organized into small groups. Each group had its own king. One person might have ruled all the groups. There were also priests, warriors, traders, and farmers. Farmers grew crops in the fields. The Maya believed in many gods and goddesses.

KEY DATES

1500 B.C.	first Mayan groups settle in what is now Mexico
A.D. 300–900	Mayan Empire grows; cities are built; the Mayan people trade
A.D. 900	Mayan groups break up
A.D. 1520	Spanish move into the area

Mayan step pyramids, like this one, were used to worship the gods and goddesses.

What are the Maya known for?

The Maya built stone, step pyramids. They made beautiful pottery. They used picture writing called hieroglyphics.

What happened to the Maya?

The Mayan Empire began to fall apart in about A.D. 900. No one knows why this happened. They may have been invaded by other tribes. Some Maya moved south. They were taken over by the Spanish. There are still Mayan people in most of the countries in Central America.

Measurement

see also: Calendar, Number, Time

Measurement tells the size of an object or the number of things in a group. Measurement is also a way to find the right size or the right number. Measurement makes sure that things like cakes and medicines are the same every time.

The first measurements

The first measurements were units that could be found anywhere. Parts of the human body were used for measuring in ancient Egypt. For example, a cubit was the length of an arm from the tip of the middle finger to the elbow. Not everyone is the same size, so these measurements were not always the same.

The metric system

About 200 years ago the metric system was first used in France. Now the metric system is used around the world.

DIFFERENT METRIC UNITS
Length: kilometers (km), meters (m), centimeters (cm), millimeters (mm)   10 mm = 1 cm   100 cm = 1 m   1000 m = 1 km
Mass: metric tons (t), kilograms (kg), grams (g), milligrams (mg)   1000 mg = 1 g   1000 g = 1 kg   1000 kg = 1 t
Capacity: liters (l), milliliters (ml)   1000 ml = 1 l
Time: seconds, minutes, hours, days, months   60 seconds = 1 minute   60 minutes = 1 hour   24 hours = 1 day   28–31 days = 1 month   12 months = 1 year

This diamond is being measured. The gauge tells how wide it is.

DID YOU KNOW?

Some old units are still used for special things. The weight of diamonds are measured in carats. A carat is based on the weight of a carob bean.

Metal

see also: Magnet, Meteor, Rock

Metals are solid materials. Metals can be made into shapes. Some metals are strong, shiny, and hard. Other metals are weak, dull, and soft. Most metals are found in rocks in the ground. Rocks containing metal are called ores.

Properties of metals

Electricity and heat pass through metal. This is called conduction. Most electric wires are made of the metal called copper. Copper conducts electricity. Copper can be bent and stretched into wires.

Metals can be mixed together. Mixed metals are called alloys. An alloy can be better than each metal by itself. Bronze is an alloy made of copper and tin. Bronze is stronger than copper or tin.

Gold is a valuable metal. It has been used for thousands of years. This gold mask covered the mummy of Egyptian pharaoh Tutankhamen.

Using metals today

Important metals are iron alloys, copper, and aluminum. Many alloys containing iron are called steel. Steel is very strong and heavy. It is used to make skyscrapers, ships, and cars. Aluminum is strong and light. It is used to make pots and pans and drink cans.

Steel is heated until it is red-hot. Then the steel is rolled into shape.

Metamorphosis

see also: Amphibian, Insect, Life Cycle

The word "metamorphosis" means change. Metamorphosis is what happens to some insects as they go through different stages in their lives.

The metamorphosis of a butterfly

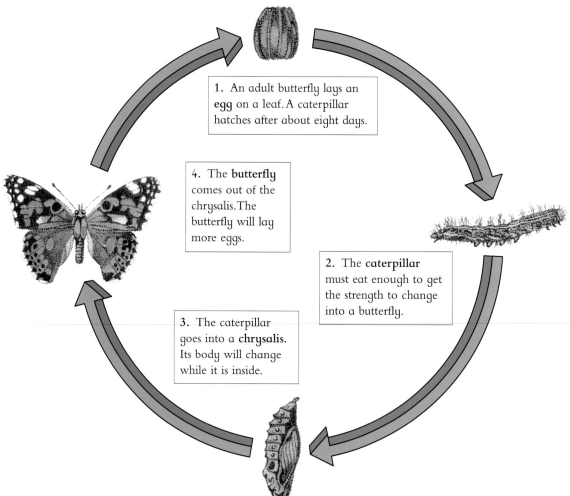

1. An adult butterfly lays an **egg** on a leaf. A caterpillar hatches after about eight days.

4. The **butterfly** comes out of the chrysalis. The butterfly will lay more eggs.

2. The **caterpillar** must eat enough to get the strength to change into a butterfly.

3. The caterpillar goes into a **chrysalis**. Its body will change while it is inside.

Fast and slow changes

All insects and some amphibians go through a metamorphosis. This change is complete and sudden for insects like butterflies. For other insects, such as grasshoppers, the change is slower.

A grasshopper changes its skin four or five times as it grows. It becomes more like an adult grasshopper each time it changes. The new skin is soft and wet. The new skin gets harder as it dries.

Meteor

see also: Earth, Solar System

A meteor is a piece of rock or metal. It flies through space. Meteors that enter the earth's atmosphere are sometimes called shooting or falling stars.

Watching for meteors

The earth meets millions of meteors every day as it moves through space. These meteors can sometimes be seen in the sky on a clear, dark night. A bright meteor may leave a glowing trail behind it. Some meteors are in groups. The group might be seen as a meteor shower. These showers often come from the tails of comets.

As a meteor enters the earth's atmosphere, it burns up. This causes the bright streak of light in the sky.

DID YOU KNOW?

Some meteor showers last a few days. They can be seen at the same time and in the same place in the sky every year.

This meteorite crater in Arizona is nearly a mile across. It was made about 25 thousand years ago.

Meteorites

Meteorites are meteors that reach the earth. They did not burn up in the earth's atmosphere. Meteorites may be pieces of other planets. They may come from other solar systems. Most meteorites are the size of dust. Sometimes a big meteorite will hit the ground very hard. The hole it makes is called a crater. Many giant meteorites hit the earth billions of years ago. Most of the craters that they made were worn down by wind and rain. Some of these craters filled with water. The moon has been hit by meteorites. The moon's craters can be seen from Earth.

Mexico

see also: Aztecs, Maya, North America

Mexico is a country in North America. There are mountains in the west and near the Gulf of Mexico. There is high, flat land between the mountains. This land is warm and dry. The coastal lowlands are hot and wet.

Living in Mexico

Many Mexicans live in the cities. They work in businesses, factories, and with tourists. Farmers grow corn, beans, and vegetables for their families. Big farms grow cotton, coffee, and fruit to sell in Mexico and in other countries.

Mexicans are a mix of Native Americans and people who came from Spain. Some of the foods, like enchiladas, come from the Indian cultures.

Almost anything can be bought in Mexico's open markets. This stall sells fruit and vegetables.

North America

FACT FILE

PEOPLE	Mexicans
POPULATION	almost 105 million
MAIN LANGUAGES	Spanish
CAPITAL CITY	Mexico City
MONEY	Peso
HIGHEST MOUNTAIN	Pico de Orizaba–18,707 feet
LONGEST RIVER	Rio Bravo Del Norte–1,885 miles

Michigan

see also: United States of America

Michigan is a state in the northern United States of America. It is divided into two peninsulas. Both peninsulas are on the Great Lakes. The Upper Peninsula has hills and mountains. The Lower Peninsula is flat and has good soil for farming. Winters in Michigan are very cold.

Life in Michigan

Many people work in Michigan's factories. The first automobile factories in the nation were in Detroit, Flint, and Pontiac. During World War II, the factories made tanks, trucks, and airplanes. Thousands of African Americans came to Michigan to work in the factories.

Michigan's factories still produce more cars than those in any other state.

Car engines are being built on this assembly line in Detroit, Michigan.

DID YOU KNOW?

Michigan's two peninsulas are separated by the Straits of Mackinac. The 3,800-foot Mackinac Bridge crosses the strait. It is one of the longest suspension bridges in the world.

Factory workers in Michigan also make tools, airplane parts, furniture, and breakfast cereals. Outside of the cities, people work in tourism, farming, and forestry. They mine iron ore used to make steel.

Michigan

FACT FILE

BECAME A STATE .. 1837 (26th state)

LAND AREA .... 56,804 square miles

. . . . (22nd largest land area)

POPULATION 10,079,985

. . . . (8th most populated state)

OTHER NAMES..... Wolverine State, Great Lakes State

CAPITAL CITY ..... Lansing

Middle Ages

see also: Castle, Cathedral, Knight

The Middle Ages is a time in the history of Europe. It is the time between the fall of the Roman Empire and the Renaissance.

What happened in the Middle Ages?

At the beginning of the Middle Ages, small areas of Europe each had their own rulers. Then most of Europe became Christian. Europe was united by religion. People began to build towns and cities. They traded with each other. There was less fighting. Europe became richer. Europeans built cathedrals, castles, and universities. At the beginning of the Middle Ages, only people who were part of the church could read and write. By the end of the Middle Ages, many more people could read and write.

What happened next?

The Middle Ages did not suddenly stop. One by one, countries moved into the time called the Renaissance.

By the end of the Middle Ages, more people lived in towns and cities. These people are making hay outside the city walls.

KEY DATES

A.D. 476 .... fall of the Roman Empire	A.D. 1100 .... universities begin
A.D. 800 .... most of Europe unites under Emperor Charlemagne	A.D. 1130 .... first school for doctors opens
	A.D. 1330 .... Renaissance begins in Italy
A.D. 1066 .. William of Normandy conquers England	A.D. 1450 .... Renaissance spreads through Europe

Migration

see also: Animal

Migration is a kind of journey made by an animal. It can be a journey to find a mate. It can be a journey to find food. It can be a journey to find the right kind of weather. Different kinds of animals migrate. Sometimes people migrate.

Why migrate?

Most migrating animals leave an area when winter comes. They travel to warmer places. They may have longer days and plenty of food in the warmer place. The animals leave the winter area when spring comes. They return to their summer home.

Young salmon are born in rivers. Then they swim out to sea. They stay in the sea for a year or two. The salmon return to the river where they were born. They swim up the river against the current.

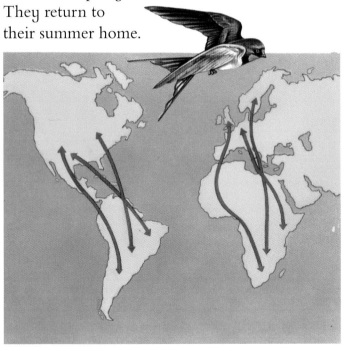

Migrating swallows leave their homes in the fall. These birds spend the winter in Africa or South America. They fly back home in the spring. Each way of their journey can be as much as 6,200 miles.

Mining

see also: Metal, Rock

Mining means digging things out of the earth. Most mining takes rocks, minerals, metals, oil, gas, and coal from the earth.

Types of mining

Rocks near the surface of the ground can be dug from a pit. This is called strip mining. Giant mechanical shovels scoop up the rocks. Other things are mined from deep under the ground. A mine shaft is dug down until it reaches the layer to be mined. Then explosives, drills, and giant cutters are used to do the mining. Oil and gas are mined by drilling holes deep into the ground. Then the oil or gas comes up to the surface on its own, or it is pumped up.

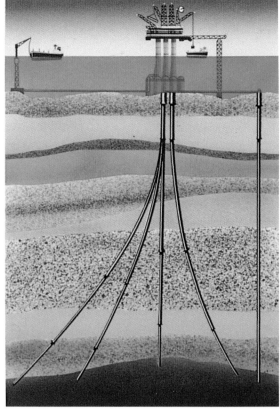

Oil and gas are pumped up from deep under the sea floor.

Copper is mined from this strip mine in Arizona.

People and mining

People have dug mines for thousands of years. Mining gets people what they want from the earth. Salt is mined to use in cooking and preserving food. Coal, gas, and oil are mined to use as fuel to make electricity and heat. They are also fuel for transportation.

DID YOU KNOW?

Some precious metals and rocks are used to make jewelry. Silver, gold, diamonds, and rubies all come from mines.

Minnesota

see also: United States of America

Minnesota is a state in the northern United States of America. The state borders the Great Lakes in the northeast. The northern half of Minnesota has lakes, forests, and rocky land. The southern half of the state has rolling plains with good soil for farming. Minnesota has very cold winters and lots of snow.

Life in Minnesota

Minneapolis and St. Paul are the state's largest cities. They are known as the "Twin Cities." The Twin Cities sit opposite each other on the Mississippi River. About half the state's population lives in the Twin Cities. Most of them work in services. They serve in stores, restaurants, and banks. They work in offices of trade and transportation companies.

The city of Minneapolis sits on the Mississippi River.

DID YOU KNOW?

Minnesota is sometimes called the "Land of 10,000 Lakes." In fact, there are about 11,000 lakes there. People go to the lakes to swim, boat, fish, and waterski. In winter, they skate, ski, and sled on the frozen lakes.

Outside of the cities, farmers in Minnesota grow lots of wheat, corn, and rye. They produce eggs, milk, and butter. Miners in the north supply 70 percent of the iron ore mined in the United States.

FACT FILE

Minnesota

BECAME A STATE...	1858 (32nd state)
LAND AREA.........	79,610 square miles (14th largest land area)
POPULATION.......	5,059,375 (21st most populated state)
OTHER NAMES.....	North Star State, Gopher State, Land of 10,000 Lakes
CAPITAL CITY......	St. Paul

Mississippi

see also: Delta, United States of America

Mississippi is a state in the southern United States of America. The land in the west is river delta. The rest of the state is prairie and woodland. There are hills, grasslands, and pine forests. The weather in Mississippi is warm and rainy.

Life in Mississippi

Farming is important in Mississippi. Cotton and soybeans both grow well in the rich soil of the delta. Farmers also grow rice, sugar cane, and corn. Fish farmers raise catfish in ponds. Fishermen and women bring in shrimp and oysters from the Gulf of Mexico.

About half the people in Mississippi live in rural areas. Some of them travel to work in the state's cities. Many people in Mississippi now work in factories.

A cotton field stretches along the Mississippi River delta.

DID YOU KNOW?

For many years, large farms called plantations covered Mississippi's farmland. Slaves worked growing cotton on the plantations. Many of the old plantation houses in Mississippi have been preserved.

The factories in the state produce chemicals, plastics, and wood products.

Mississippi

FACT FILE

BECAME A STATE...	1817 (20th state)
LAND AREA.........	46,907 square miles (31st largest land area)
POPULATION	2,881,281 (31st most populated state)
OTHER NAME	Magnolia State
CAPITAL CITY	Jackson

Missouri

see also: United States of America

Missouri is a state in the central United States of America. Missouri shares its border with eight other states. Much of the land in Missouri is hills and plains. There are mountains and valleys in the southern part of the state. The state has a mild climate. Sometimes there are tornadoes in the spring and summer.

The Ozarks are colored pink by the sunset.

In the past

The two longest rivers in the United States meet in Missouri. The rivers are the Mississippi and the Missouri. The rivers have been important in history. Native Americans traveled on them to trade with other tribes. Explorers from Europe used the rivers in the 1600s and 1700s. In 1804, Lewis and Clark made a great journey along the Missouri River from St. Louis.

DID YOU KNOW?

In 1811 and 1812, a series of powerful earthquakes rocked New Madrid, Missouri. People felt the tremors a thousand miles away.

Life in Missouri

Many people work in trade and transportation. Others work in manufacturing. Factories in Missouri make transportation equipment and beverages. People in Missouri also mine lead and raise crops and livestock.

Missouri

FACT FILE

BECAME A STATE	1821 (24th state)
LAND AREA	68,886 square miles (18th largest land area)
POPULATION	5,704,484 (17th most populated state)
OTHER NAME	Show Me State
CAPITAL CITY	Jefferson City

Mollusk

see also: Animal, Invertebrate

Mollusks are invertebrates. They are animals with soft bodies. There are more than 70 thousand kinds of mollusks. Some mollusks have shells. The shells of cuttlefish and squid are inside their bodies.

Mollusk families

All mollusks lay eggs. Most female mollusks lay eggs on plants or in the water. The eggs hatch on their own. The babies find food for themselves.

Some mollusks look after their eggs. The female giant octopus protects her eggs for six months. She never leaves her nest, not even to find food for herself.

This large clam lives on the bottom of the sea.

Where mollusks live

Some mollusks, such as some snails and slugs, live on land. They crawl over leaves and eat the leaves. Squid and octopuses live in saltwater seas. They eat fish and other water creatures. Shellfish live on rocks under the sea. They eat tiny animals and plants called plankton from the seawater. There are freshwater clams and oysters living in rivers and lakes. They eat tiny freshwater creatures.

There are eight plates in the shell of this mollusk. It is called a chiton.

DID YOU KNOW?

The largest mollusk in the world is the giant squid. It can grow as long as 50 feet. That is longer than a bus.

Money

see also: Haiti

Money is used by people to buy things they need. People are given money in exchange for things they sell or for work they do.

Why use money?

People did not use money hundreds of years ago. They swapped things with each other. This is called bartering. Later, people used shells, cocoa beans, or bits of metal to swap for the things they needed. This was easier than bartering.

Real money

The first real money was metal coins. Then governments began to make paper money. Every country makes its own money. The coins and paper money look different. They have different names.

Plastic money

A credit card or charge card is a plastic card. It has a name and an account number on it. The card can be used to pay for things. The credit card company pays the business. Then the credit card company collects the money from the person whose name is on the card. Some people call credit cards "plastic money."

Here is money from Uganda, Brazil, the United States, the United Kingdom, and Australia.

DID YOU KNOW?

Checks are a kind of money. Checks can be filled in with whatever amount of money is needed. The person who writes the check has to have that amount of money in the bank.

Monkey

see also: Ape, Mammal

A monkey is a mammal. It belongs to the same group of mammals as apes and human beings. They live in Africa, Asia, and South America. Monkeys have strong arms and legs. They are good climbers and runners.

Monkey families

Monkeys live in groups called troops. The strongest male monkey is the leader. Each troop has several female monkeys and their babies. A female monkey usually has one baby at a time.

MONKEY FACTS

NUMBER OF KINDS	about 400
COLOR	usually brown, black, white, or gray
HEIGHT	5 inches to 3 feet
WEIGHT	2 oz. to 100 lbs.
STATUS	some types are endangered
LIFE SPAN	up to 18 years
ENEMIES	birds, snakes, larger animals, people

fur for keeping warm

strong tail to use as an extra arm for climbing and for balance

hands have fingers and feet have toes for holding and picking up things

a baboon

This baby squirrel monkey is with its mother and a brother or sister.

PLANT, INSECT, AND MEAT EATER

Monkeys move from place to place. They eat fruit and leaves. Monkeys peel fruit with their fingers and teeth. Some monkeys also eat insects and small mammals.

Montana

see also: United States of America

Montana is a state in the northwestern United States of America. The eastern part of the state is on the Great Plains. It has hills and grasslands. The western part of the state is in the Rocky Mountains. It has high mountains. The weather in Montana is dry and sunny. It is very cold in winter.

Life in Montana

Montana is a large state with no really big cities. The biggest is Billings, where fewer than 100 thousand people live. There are seven Indian reservations in the state. They are home to thousands of Native Americans.

There is lots of space in Montana for raising livestock and growing crops. There are many cattle ranches and sheep farms. Farmers also raise wheat

Mountains rise up in Glacier National Park, Montana.

DID YOU KNOW?

A famous battle took place in Montana in 1876. It was the Battle of the Little Bighorn, or "Custer's Last Stand." Cheyenne, Sioux, and Arapaho warriors defeated U.S. soldiers in the battle.

and barley. Mines still produce valuable resources for Montana. Today, people mine more coal and oil than metals.

Montana

FACT FILE

MONTANA

BECAME A STATE...	1889 (41st state)
LAND AREA.........	145,552 square miles
	(4th largest land area)
POPULATION	918 thousand
	(44th most populated state)
OTHER NAME	Treasure State
CAPITAL CITY	Helena

Moon

see also: Earth, Solar System, Space Exploration, Sun

The moon is a big ball of rock. It travels around the earth. Its path is called an orbit. It is the brightest thing in the night sky.

The moon's phases

Every month the moon goes through phases. First it looks like a thin crescent. Then it seems to grow to a full circle. Finally, it shrinks back again. The moon takes about 29½ days for each orbit around the earth.

The same side of the moon always faces the earth. The moon does not give out light. It is lit by the sun's light reflecting off the moon's surface.

On the moon

The patterns that can be seen on the moon are its mountains, craters, and plains. Most of the moon's craters are billions of years old. There is no air or water on the moon to wear away the mountains and craters. In July 1969, the U.S. space mission *Apollo 11* flew to the moon. The commander, Neil Armstrong, was the first person to walk on the moon.

MOON FACTS

SIZE	2,160 miles across
DISTANCE	about 239 thousand miles from Earth
HOTTEST PART	266°F
COLDEST PART	–280°F

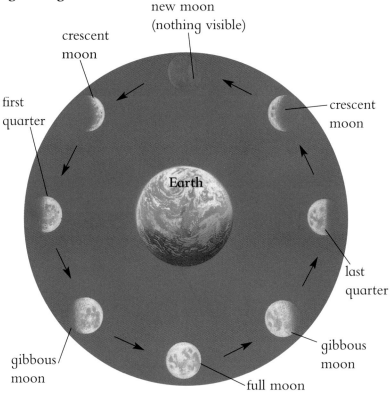

The moon only seems to change shape. This is because the light shining on it from the sun is blocked by the earth. This picture shows the phases of the moon as it orbits the earth.

DID YOU KNOW?

Other planets in our solar system also have orbiting moons. Saturn has the most moons. It has at least 31.

Moose

see also: Arctic, Deer

The moose is a mammal. It is the largest deer in the world. Moose live in forests in the northern parts of the world. Moose walk into lakes during the summer. They eat the water plants and cool off in the water.

Moose families

The male moose is called a bull. The female moose is called a cow. Male moose live on their own. They fight over the females every autumn. The female moose has one or two babies in the spring. These babies are called calves. Calves may stay with their mother for a year.

thick, furry coat for keeping warm

a male moose

MOOSE FACTS

NUMBER OF KINDS	6
COLOR	brown with lighter brown legs
LENGTH	up to 10 feet
HEIGHT	up to 8 feet
WEIGHT	880 to 1,800 lbs.
STATUS	common
LIFE SPAN	about 20 years
ENEMIES	wolves, cougars, people

males have large antlers for fighting

sensitive nose for smelling danger

males have a growth of skin and hair called a bell

PLANT EATER

A moose eats only plants. It eats water plants and grass. Moose eat many plants each day.

This female moose is grazing with her young calf.

Morocco

see also: Africa, Desert

Morocco is a country on the northwest coast of Africa. Morocco has mountain ranges and a high, flat area. It has some desert. The coast has hot summers and mild, wet winters.

Living in Morocco

Many people live in the country. Most are farmers. They grow citrus fruit, vegetables, wheat, and barley. Some people work with tourists. Others work in mining and fishing.

Moroccans eat *couscous*. It is made from wheat. The wheat is cracked and then cooked by steaming. Almost anything can be eaten with *couscous*. Stews made of spicy meat and vegetables are favorites.

The covered markets are called bazaars. Whole streets of shops might all sell the same thing. These shops sell things made of brass.

DID YOU KNOW?

Computers are used to help farmers in Morocco. The computers run machines that water the crops.

Africa

FACT FILE

PEOPLE	Moroccans
POPULATION	about 32 million
MAIN LANGUAGES	Arabic, Berber
CAPITAL CITY	Rabat
MONEY	Dirham
HIGHEST MOUNTAIN	Jebel Toubkal–13,670 feet
LONGEST RIVER	Oued Moulouya–354 miles

Mosquito

see also: Fly, Insect

A mosquito is an insect. It is a small fly. Mosquitoes are found all over the world. They live in warm and wet places. Many mosquitoes carry diseases.

MOSQUITO FACTS

NUMBER OF KINDS	3,000
COLOR	brownish
LENGTH	less than one inch
STATUS	common
LIFE SPAN	less than one year
ENEMIES	birds, bats, fish, people

Mosquito families

Mosquitoes do not look after their eggs or babies. A female mosquito lays her eggs in still or slow-flowing water.

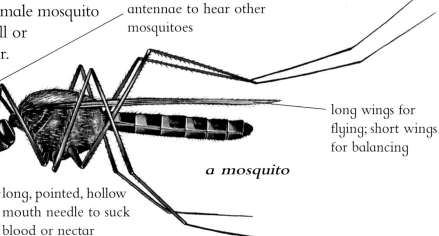

antennae to hear other mosquitoes

long wings for flying; short wings for balancing

a mosquito

long, pointed, hollow mouth needle to suck blood or nectar

A mosquito grows from an egg to an adult mosquito in stages. The eggs hatch into little wormlike larvae. The larvae live in water. A fully-grown larva forms a covering to become a pupa. Then the adult mosquito comes out of the pupa.

PLANT, INSECT, AND MEAT EATER

A mosquito larva eats tiny animals in the water. Adult female mosquitoes drink the blood of humans or animals. Male mosquitoes drink nectar or plant juice.

This mosquito is coming out of its pupa.

Moss

see also: Plant

A moss is a small, green plant. It grows best in damp places. Mosses usually grow close together. They form a mat. They grow all over the world. They do not grow in the sea. They are mostly found on smooth rocks, on trees, and on the ground. Mosses do not have flowers.

The life of moss

A new moss plant grows in two stages. First a male sperm and female egg combine. They grow into a long stalk. The stalk has a capsule at the end. Inside the capsule are thousands of spores. The spores might grow into new moss plants.

Many insects live in mosses. Birds sometimes line their nests with moss. Moss holds water like a sponge. This stops water from draining away. Peat is a spongy kind of soil. It forms from the broken-down remains of peat moss.

MOSS FACTS

NUMBER OF
KINDS .... 12 thousand
HEIGHT .... up to 6 inches

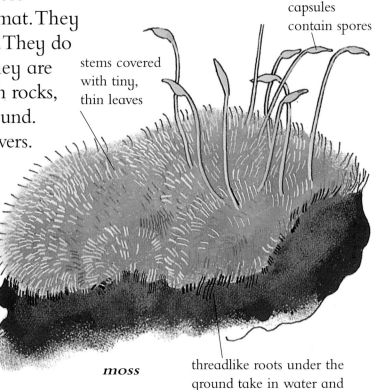

capsules contain spores

stems covered with tiny, thin leaves

moss

threadlike roots under the ground take in water and hold moss in place

Moss grows in cool, dark places. This hair moss has green and red leaves.

Moth

see also: Butterfly, Caterpillar, Insect, Metamorphosis

A moth is an insect. It has large wings. A moth begins life as a caterpillar. It later changes into a moth. Moths are found all over the world. They fly mostly in the evening or at night.

How moths live

A moth caterpillar eats enough food to become very plump. Then the caterpillar spins a cocoon around itself. It becomes a chrysalis. The caterpillar changes into a moth inside the chrysalis.

Each kind of moth has a way to avoid enemies. The tiger moth tastes terrible to birds. The buff-tip moth looks like a twig. This helps it hide. The eyed-hawk moth has large eye patterns on its wings. This frightens off enemies.

MOTH FACTS	
NUMBER OF	
KINDS	more than 100 thousand
SIZE	less than an inch to 8 inches across
STATUS.	some species threatened
LIFE SPAN	up to 3 years
ENEMIES	birds, bats, reptiles, frogs

a luna moth

feelers act like eyes and nose to find other moths

tiny scales make colorful wing patterns

veins hold the wings flat and make the wings strong

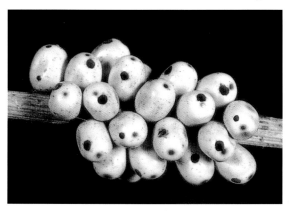

PLANT EATER

Moths sip sweet juice from flowers and rotting fruit. They eat using a mouth tube. They roll up the mouth tube when they are not drinking.

The caterpillars have hatched from these fox moth eggs.

Motorcycle

see also: Bicycle, Transportation

A motorcycle is a vehicle with two wheels.
It carries one or two people. A motorcycle
is pushed by the energy from an engine.

The first motorcycles

Motorcycles were invented more
than one hundred years ago. The first
motorcycles were bicycles with an
engine. They were very slow and
dangerous. Later more powerful
engines were invented. Motorcycles
with the new engines could go faster.
They could reach speeds of 100 miles
per hour. These motorcycles were
heavy and hard to steer. Today
motorcycles are more comfortable to
ride. The frames and engines are
lighter. Softer tires absorb the bumps.

*Modern motorcycles can travel
very fast. They have room for a
passenger to sit behind the driver.*

*This motorcycle and sidecar were the
latest thing at a motorshow in 1930.
The sidecar had a sliding roof.*

How motorcycles are used

All over the world, motorcycles are
used for transportation. They do not
get stuck in traffic. They use less fuel.
They do not cost much to run.
Motorcycle riders can get wet and
cold in bad weather. Motorcycles are
not very safe on icy roads or snow.

MOTORCYCLE FIRSTS

INVENTED	1869
FIRST MADE	1885
FIRST TRACK RACES	1897
FIRST CROSS-COUNTRY RACE	1907